At the Foot of the Cross!

This is My Story

Carolyn Blake

At the Foot of The Cross: My Story: Carolyn Blake

Copyright © 2018 by Carolyn Blake
All rights reserved. This book or any portion thereof
may not be reproduced or used in any manner whatsoever
without the express written permission of the publisher
except for the use of brief quotations in a book review.

Printed in the United States of America

First Printing

ISBN 978-1-943284-22-1 (pbk.)

ISBN 978-1-943284-23-8 (ebk)

A2Z Books Publishing
Lithonia, GA 30058

www.A2ZBooksPublishing.com

Manufactured in the United States of America

A2Z Books Publishing has allowed this work to remain exactly as the author intended, verbatim.

Dedication

This book is dedicated to the memory of my grandparents John and Mamie Simmons. To my mom (Dorothy), my dad (Aaron), & my step dad (Clarence).

The legacy of writing is left to my husband (James) to my children (Aretha and James Jr.) my grandchildren (Terry, Blake, and Jaden).

This book is credited to "The Village" Red Top and my church family New Hope Baptist Church

My many Family and friends

The ultimate dedication is to Jesus Christ the Center of my Joy the Creator of Carolyn Gibbs Blake

Contents

Dedication 3

Contents 4

Introduction 1

Chapter 1: At the Foot of the Cross 3

Chapter 2: A Stirred Spirit 13

Chapter 3: Diminish to Replenish 19

Chapter 4: You Put Me on the Back Burner 25

Chapter 5: God was preparing me 31

Chapter 6: The Care Taker 37

Chapter 7: This is my Story 43

Conclusion 47

Contact Info 59

Introduction

In this book, I pray that you find hope, faith, and inspiration.

I pray that you are granted peace that surpasses all understanding.

Make yourself available to the remodeling of the potter's wheel.

Begin to bless the Lord at all times, Let His praise continually be in your mouth.

Love, Carolyn

Chapter 1:
At the Foot of the Cross

CAROLYN BLAKE

Psalm 139:1 – Oh Lord you have searched me and you know me.

On September 7, 2015, my life was changed completely and for the better. Because God knew me before I was formed in my mother's womb, what happened did not catch Him by surprise. However, for me, one single unplanned move caused me to encounter a tear in an artery to my heart, which later was called a CABG. That day began my encounter at the foot of the cross. This day would test my faith, my love, my provision, security and peace of mind in Jesus whom I called by name as long as I could remember.

Before I knew it, my family was gathered around me listening to the doctor's report, and what needed to be done. Within hours, the surgery was done, but before that decision-making time, I looked at one person to the next. My niece, my husband, my daughter (she made it from her home which was hours away it seemed like in an hour), but I felt her anointed warm hands touch my forehead. She was putting forth the smile she always put forth in the time of pain, hurt, crisis and doing what needed to be done.

Then I thought of my son, who was incarcerated at the time of this writing. How he made his usual call to check on us to find out that his mom was headed to a life-threating surgery and he could not be there. What if? I wondered as I shook my head. I immediately shook the negative thoughts out of my mind as I was reminded that God thought I was worth saving. Thirty-nine stripes were for my healing. "Thank You, God." I made it through the Surgery, and let me tell you about the power of prayer in the name of Jesus.

At one point I did not know how, but at least ten people was in my room at once. I received cards, flowers, calls, and visitations. Lying at the foot of the cross showed me just how God died that I might live. He bore my sickness, took the sting of death away so that I may live to see and receive light from the darkness I thought had disrupted my life. It was overwhelming to see friends, family, co-

AT THE FOOT OF THE CROSS

workers, church families, children and babies come to nurse me back to life. My caregivers at the hospital spoke life into my circumstance. I remember the Chaplin asking me my favorite scripture. I told her Psalm 27- The Lord is my Light and my Salvation, whom shall I fear?

She went and printed it up and blessed me with a copy. So, at the foot of the cross there is compassion, love, humbleness, concern, togetherness.

At the foot of the cross, you receive a personal relationship with the Father. God invites you to look unto the hill from whence cometh your help (Psalm 121), at the foot of the cross an abundant relationship is made between you and God. When you are weak, He makes you strong; he becomes the Center of Your Joy. The Revelation and truth that you receive through the Holy Spirit will amaze you. I know it did for me. The Holy Spirit inspired me to put my heart and thoughts on paper. *At the Cross, at the Cross where I first saw the light and the burden of my heart rolled away, it was there by faith, I received my sight and now I am happy all the day.* A song I grew up hearing my grandmother singing, but now understand what she was singing about. She was delivered, set free because she laid at the foot of the cross.

It is amazing how complicated things have gotten or we've made it to be. We spend so much time trying to prove ourselves or prove a point, until we forget God's got it. His word proves it in Proverbs 3:5-6, Trust in the Lord with all Thine heart and lean not to your own understanding, but in all thy ways acknowledge Him and He shall direct your path. Trusting is faith, it's believing, it's taking God at his word. When we begin to give God the wheel and let him drive, there are no detours, wrong way, do not enter, or U-turns. You begin to trust this song. Lead me, guide me, along the way, Lord if you lead me I shall not stray, Lord let me walk each day with Thee, Lead me oh Lord Lead me.

CAROLYN BLAKE

God has a way of refocusing your life. You are not burden by diseases in your life. Distractions takes your focus from the cross, from the source. He says to come unto me all ye that are heavy laden and I will give you rest. No pretense, no hidden agendas. Just allowing God to love you. At the cross, Jesus opened His arms to give you love, goodness, mercy and blessings. You are ahead when you lay at the foot of the cross. Rest in Him and let Him bring you out. The blood on the doorpost was in a symbol of the cross, how he hung, bled and died, so that we are given the power God's power and authority to defeat the enemy at his game plan.

That plan is to mess with our minds, and if he gains our minds, he will then have our mind and entire being. I've learned that the enemy uses the same enticing tactics over and over and over again in different ways, through different circumstance and persons. However, if any man needs wisdom he should ask. So, I ask for a spirit of discernment everyday so I can be covered under the mandate of the Holy Spirit. I need God to give me power, and to use His power you have to be in tune to Him through a personal relationship. God will meet you right where you are if you make yourself a willing vessel, willing to be taught, led, convinced, convicted, humbled and obedient unto His will and way. Whatever we need from God He has already given unto us. Read Ephesians 6th Chapter. He's made the way of Escape.

I look back over my life even as a child and see that God had begun to mold me and make me for the journey at hand. My grandparents raised my brothers and me. Our parents were divorced, so my brokenness began at an early age. At our age we realized that we were different from others, but yet the same as many. We found ourselves being raised by God-fearing grandparents with great beliefs and work values. My brothers and I were aware that they were older and we also were aware that our mother was an alcoholic. Later, as I found out why and what cause a beautiful woman of their children

AT THE FOOT OF THE CROSS

to give up on hopes and dreams but never on her love and children, my respect and love for my mother became deeper and deeper. I was introduced to looking beyond others faults and weakness at an early age. I do admit as I grew older and saw unjust things happen, people who criticized, bullied, laughed, turned there heads, for a time my love and respect was in a valley experience. But, as I matured in God's love, I began to love and forgive. Personally, I believe that those two characters of God are the foundation to a happy, healthy, and prosperous life.

Most people go day by day doing the same things day in and day out. I know because I am still there. So, I'm asking God to help set up a strategic, purposeful plan for my day to day connection with him. So that he can guide me to a fulfilling day, week, month and year. I am believing that in our same day to day operation, He will allow us to impact someone or something in that day to cause us to feel that our day was purpose driven. Our day to day can cause us to feel bound and that's not a good feeling, do you agree? God is a God of purpose, one of peace, one of grace. His will for us is to have life, and have it more abundantly.

God is concerned about every area of our lives. It's about time for us to set aside time to evaluate what is my hindrance in my day that keeping me from becoming that effective Kingdom minded solider servant that God declares for me to become. I want to help somebody along the way, so that my living shall not be in vain. Where can I go today to find solitude? To the park, at the library, to my war room? Maybe outside to enjoy God's open peace. Looking at the earth and the fullness thereof. We need to allow ourselves to dwell in the secret place of the most high. (Psalms 91). Oh my, just to concentrate on being in an abiding place in a relationship with the almighty. Where you draw strength, guidance, wisdom and hope. The more I write, the more I see God's revelation of what He wants to do for you and me. Here, I see that, thank you Lord! Our hope is built on nothing less than Jesus Blood and His righteousness. Yes, His blood that He shed for us, to have a chance to get to know him. His righteousness, his healing deliverance, miraculous miracles and power. A chance to touch the hem of his garment is a chance to receive healing and feel his promises come to life.

I am convinced that our flesh can over power our emotions. It can psychically tear us down because of what we see. We see debt, we see our families torn, we look at Church people not Kingdom people, and we look at our jobs for our source, our relationships for our strength. Don't let our religious tradition cancel the promises of God in our lives. Use God's words as your weapons, your worship as your praise, your songs as your peace, your prayers as your keeper and your armor as your defense. In Matthew 6:5 Go into your secret closet, shut the door and prayer to thy father in secret. Shut the enemy out. Make your request known unto the Lord. So now, in our secret closet, the enemy will try to infiltrate you, take your mind off your request, your prayer but as you begin to praise Him, thank Him, for all His blessings, all his protection, all His deliverance there is no room for Satan to attack but instead flee as you call on the name of Jesus. You at this point have taken on the promise of God, out of mind into reality.

Praise the Lord. Learn to see the promises of God in others, and believe your next in line. Too many times, we begin to count ourselves out because we feel we are in a "Stand Still" position. Every time something good happens, two bad things happens, but this happens because we do not put on an armor to run a race, we put it on to fight a battle. In life your race will feel like a multitude of army is on your trail and you put on a weak armor, one that you feel you have to fight because you want to see the results immediately and life circumstances and situations will feel like a weight upon your shoulders. Your spirit man will seem as though you can't break or fake a smile. Your emotions will have you anxious one day, crying

AT THE FOOT OF THE CROSS

the next. Believe this, children of God, that your race won't be a sprint. It will seem like a marathon a wilderness experience. Like the older generation, you'll begin to ask, "What have I done to make my race so hard to run?" But gird up your loins and put on your helmet, fasten your breast plate, wash your feet, put on your shoes, carry your sword and fight your good fight. For He has said to us that the Battle is not ours but it belongs to Him. So ultimately, we do not have to fight at all. But we must be armed at all times from the adversary and his schemes.

CAROLYN BLAKE

Notes

AT THE FOOT OF THE CROSS

Notes

CAROLYN BLAKE

Notes

Chapter 2:
A Stirred Spirit

CAROLYN BLAKE

It's the early morning hour, my spirit is stirred. I can't help but inquire of the Lord for his Shekinah Glory. I just have this urge to be in His presence and thank Him for his protection and provision. My soul looks back and I wonder how and why I went through and still go through struggles on this journey. But I know that it's all for God's Glory.

Proverbs 3:5-6 says, Trust in the Lord with all Thine Heart and lean not to your own understanding, but in all thy ways acknowledge Him and He shall direct your path.

Hallelujah. Trust is having faith, a new faith at that very moment in that situation. The very substance of what you need for hope. You can see what is in front of you, but deep down inside you trust God for manifestation. This communion with God, being in His presence is a blessed assurance. I can go to sleep resting and knowing that He's working it out for my good. The desires of my heart He's attending to it, working behind the scene on my behalf. That it is you Lord and it is all in your hands. I pray this encourages someone.

Your emotions can get the best of you, and it's good to let those emotions surface. If you keep hindering them, and don't face up to them, you can hinder the presence of God showing you His love, grace, mercy and compassion. It amazes me when I think about the scripture, (Matthew 6: 25-34) when it says to take no thought of what you should eat or drink for tomorrow will take care of itself. How it speaks about the birds and lilies how God make provision for them, so how much more will he do for us.

(Psalm 119:105) The word of God is a light unto our feet and lamp unto our path. It gives us hope peace and joy in solemn times and guidance when we have lost our directions. Praise God! Continually look unto the hill (Psalm 121) from whence cometh our help, know that it comes from the Lord. Think about that miracle, that protection, that provision that was super natural. No one could have work it out except Jesus. That doctor report that was turned for

AT THE FOOT OF THE CROSS

your good, that marriage that was on the verge of breaking up, that son that was release from prison not according to men time, but God. That womb that was barren but you conceived and delivered that miracle baby, that home that was in foreclosure or that car about to be repossessed. But God! But God! Not of our goodness, but because of His Divine Intervention. I almost let go, I felt like I just couldn't take life anymore, the devil thought he had me, but Jesus came and grabbed me and He held me close, so I wouldn't let go (a true song), God's mercies kept me, so I wouldn't let go. Thank you, Jesus!

When your spirit is stirred, ask God to release his discerning grace upon you, so that you won't be caught up in the snares of the enemy. The adversary is just waiting for any opportunity to cause havoc in your family, and your affairs. Petty issues hinder us experiencing joy and as Isaiah says if we keep our minds stayed of Him (God) he'll keep us in perfect peace. Petty issues don't matter, cast those thieves aside. It's a weight that God did not desire us to carry.

Ways to overlook petty issues and experience the joy and purpose of serving God and others: Philippians `1:21 instructs us to be single-minded in purpose, then there must be and order adopting God's priorities as our own. Philippians 2:5-6 Putting God first, others second, and yourself third. Next, realize that we have not yet spiritually arrived, so we have to keep moving forward spiritually to get to know more about God! Lastly, but I'm quite sure there's more to stirring the spiritual awareness, have a rejoicing mind. Don't rejoice in circumstances, but rejoice in God and His faithfulness. Philippians 4:4-5, if we fail to keep the Joy of the Lord in our personal life, it will lead to a stagnant move and a spiritual breakdown. Romans 15:13 tells us what happens when we have true joy knowing who we are and to whom we belong then we have a new identity, you have power to face life, the promise of the Holy Ghost and a new hope in Christ Jesus.

CAROLYN BLAKE

I can only tell you from experience that when you don't feel right, when you are uncomfortable you have to ask God to come in and reveal the situation. Begin to cry out to Him and intercede. All I could say is Lord whatever it is, whatever is about to happen I bind it in the name of Jesus. I ask that you cover and intervene, protect, and guide. After you finish you trust that your prayer has been heard, your intercession has covered the circumstance and believe God for the unusual interventions. It's at the foot of the cross that your burden will be lifted. Your spirit will become calm and your hope is built on Jesus.

AT THE FOOT OF THE CROSS

Notes

CAROLYN BLAKE

Notes

Chapter 3:
Diminish to Replenish

CAROLYN BLAKE

I was at home recovering from a hysterectomy. For six weeks, I was unable to lift myself up or move around too much. My husband, bless his soul, was there 24/7, and our daughter came home for two weeks. I was disappointed with our son because he was not too far to come and attend to his mother, but he could not stand to see me the way I was and not able to help in the circumstance. But how many of you know that love and forgiveness will give you a peace of mind? Then I heard in my spirit no cross no crown.

One day, after my husband had come home and checked on me for lunch, I laid still and was thinking. I laid there thinking of who called or who came by and who didn't, and got up and slowly walked outside and decided to just rest in the beauty of God's creation.

The sky, birds, blue clouds and the gentle breeze. As I closed my eyes and just listened, I heard *Diminish to Replenish*. I opened my eyes, looked around, and repeated Diminish to Replenish? Lord what are you trying to tell me yes, this was a God moment. Because I had cast down the thinking imagination and choose to put my mind and rest on God's creations and beauty. It was an open invitation for him to talk to me and let me know that I was in his presence and his spirit was there with me. It was his time to show himself faithful for my time of isolation and hurt.

First, he came and diminished the spirit of pain, hurt, and desolation. He diminished the gloomy cloud that hugged around me literally and replenished it with fresh air, blue skies, flying butterflies, the sounds of the birds. He replenished it with tranquility instead of anxiety or depression and gave me a blessed assurance that Jesus is mine. He's been there all the time, but he was waiting for me to cast my cares on him and not what it seemed or felt.

This is a constant Journey everyone and anything that comes after you to steal your joy, your peace, your family, your finance you must believe that God and his word is there just waiting for us to ask him and use the Basic Instruction for daily living to guide us to true living.

AT THE FOOT OF THE CROSS

Cast down and pray against the tactic of the enemy he will cause your attitude to flare up and if you are not rooted and grounded enough in your relationship with God you will fight a losing battle. Let's think about word; once said it can't be taken back. It can produce confidence or devastation and in my family, it has caused many emotional disparities. I think back to my grandmother's time, there were no demeaning words in our household not from them, we just got our butts torn up.

We did not get mad if they did not or could not make an event or come to school, we held whatever we felt or wanted to say under our breath. If we did not want to go to Sunday School or church, we did not have a choice. We had to go rather they were going or not. Just because we went to school we did not make them feel like they weren't knowledgeable of what they already knew. One thing I can say now that I am a mother and grandmother: they had the spirit, they were so connected with God that the little education they had could not touch the Holy Spirit that was within them.

Now because I was raised with the love and the value of God, even though I stepped aside here and there, once I was laid down at the foot of the cross, my discernment for situations, people and tactics has been elevated by the Holy Spirit. I've learned to shut up and let God reveal His answer and handiwork. I do this with my children, grandchildren, job, and church people even with my finances. I won't write and tell you that I don't get concerned but I know where to go in prayer and ask God to fix it. He is for that you know and He wants good things for His children as he uses them for His good pleasure. I'm not saying that I've got it all right. I still battle with thinking I'm right. I still battle with talking without listening. I still have a fight with anxiety and patience. Oh, and I also deal with people who assume or try to validate me with their own opinions. I'm still guilty of judging others and trying to defend me. But I've been missing the miracle of the situation because God is love and I was made in His image. 1st John 4:7 speaks of love.

Let me encourage you to love your life, but you have to change some things to live a quality life so pray and let the word begin to diminish the anxiety, the judging, the un-forgiveness all the things that's not in the will of God. Get rid of the mess so you can rest. The song "I give myself away" oh my, just listen to the words. It will cause you to want to be used by God. Hebrews 4 tells us to rest in the Lord. When you're in the presence of the Lord you can rest and be restored, refreshed, and relieved. Jesus becomes the center of your joy. Hallelujah!! After you hear from God, do what He tells you to do.

AT THE FOOT OF THE CROSS

Notes

CAROLYN BLAKE

Notes

Chapter 4:
You Put Me on the Back Burner

July 2016 while on my way to work around 4:45am, as I was driving I was convicted by the Holy Spirit as to how I got up, washed, brushed my teeth, put on my clothing, fixed coffee and lunch for work and out the door. I was driving and heard the spirit saying, "a back-burner God". I felt so ashamed that tears came to my eyes. I didn't even thank God for waking me up, that's the least I could have done. Let alone, He gave his angels charge over me all night long. I woke up with health and strength, my home in tact, food and clothing. I had transportation outside, and a job to go to. I had all my everyday living essentials, and who gave them to me? God did it. All this for His glory, not mine.

This weighed on me so heavy at work throughout the day until one of my prayer partners said, "Ok, Carol, you've been too quiet today.

I said, "Girl, I feel so ashamed." I told her what I had done and what I heard in the spirit.

All she could say was, "Carol that is so true." As she repeated it, I guess it had an effect on her, as well. All I could hear her saying is, "My God, um, um, um! So, God's word is proven again, your testimony is not for you. I pray I'm helping someone here. Don't feel condemned because God knows our hearts. He just wants our prayer, praise and worship. He just wants a Thank you; bless your name Lord, or just the highest praise Hallelujah.

You see, I'm seeing more and more as I write this book, that the God in me is allowing me to spread the joy of the Lord, but it's not writing a picture-perfect painting of me because I am broken, but the potter can put me back together again as well as you and you and you.

Put Him on the front burner, light the burner of faith, let it begin to boil and know that you can do all things in Christ who strengthens you. God wants to be the center of our joy; the creator is there for us every second every minute of the hour. He presents himself faithful in matters that we will never ever understand, but for sure, it was not of our doing. God does not want us to go in front of Him; He wants us to follow Him. He wants us to acknowledge him for who he is. The one that is able to open doors that otherwise would be closed. He provides for every need in our lives, but too many times he is left on the back burner when we forget who did it for us.

Plainly not we ourselves, we are powerless against God and His miraculous people of faith; we cannot ignore the presence of God in our lives. He wants to bless us for who He is in our lives. And there's a blessing in obedience. Strength for this journey does not comes from the flesh. In life, we have options different choices, bad choices, good ones, both come with consequences.

In the good, there will be greater works. In the bad will be struggles to overcome. But the good news is God causes the sun to fall on the just as well as the unjust. And we all have a destiny to fulfill. Become a God chaser and let God become the chief engineer. The ultimate architecture and the conductor of every situation in your life with him driving. Again, I say there will be no U-turns.

Day by day, even in my brokenness I ask God to order my steps and direct my path. To give me my assignment for the day. To let me hear his voice not my own. To show himself mighty in whichever way he chooses. So that others may see the Jesus in me. I want Him to fill me up until I overflow. What are you asking God for? If you've placed him on the back burner for even a minute, ask his forgiveness and begin to give him the opportunity to lead and guide you daily. Yes, he is able and His word will not return unto him void. Manifestation will begin to take place in your life that will leave you and others totally amazed.

CAROLYN BLAKE

Notes

AT THE FOOT OF THE CROSS

Notes

CAROLYN BLAKE

Notes

Chapter 5:
God was preparing me

CAROLYN BLAKE

It probably will take more books to tell you how God was preparing me for so many processes, attacks, favors, provisions, protections and powers that he was and will take me through and to. I want to stop here and say, Thank you Lord! Had I not been spiritually tuned in to the instructions, guidance and convictions of the Holy Spirit, many things that took place in my family's life and mine would not have taken place. But how many of you know that when you work of yourself, that you misdirect the plan of the Father? I read from *How to Find God Living Water For Those Who Thirst* (NLT). The writer wrote from an engraving on a cathedral wall in German and it said these mind bearing thoughts what Christ spoke from Matthew 7:21. He said, "You call me master and obey me not; you call me light and see not; you call me the way and walk not; you call me life and live not; you call me wise and follow me not; you call me fair and love me not; you call me rich and ask me not; you call me eternal and see me not. If I condemn, you blame me not. This is so revealing!

God has prepared me as he calmed the storms in my life. When I was in the boat, he was right there with me. I can remember many times so to speak, waking Jesus up even though I knew he never sleeps. In my moments of fear, weary, and doubtful. Lord help me, I can't take all this. Only to hear him say: "My dear child, why are you afraid? If I did it before, I'll do it again. Where is your faith in me?"

Talk about feeling low and ashamed. Another time, when I encountered firsthand experience of a demonic spirit in my son, hearing the voice of a roaring lion trying to take my son's life out of him. I knew I had the power to defeat the enemy. But, I felt fear, so I took that oil and threw it in the name of Jesus. He immediately replied to me by saying, "Why you threw that (beep) on me?"

But God renewed my strength, and I sought that fiery dart until it was broken. I opened the door, and then told it to get out and go

AT THE FOOT OF THE CROSS

back to the pits of hell where it came from. The next morning, he was tired from what the Holy Spirit did to him.

He rested through the night, but woke up and asked, "Why is my face so greasy?" If he only knew how we wrestled with the enemy all night long. But God got the victory. Hallelujah!

As you read, the passage think about what God had prepared you for many times in your life. You might not realize it then, but at some point in your life you can say it was nobody but God. The song "Lord prepare me to be a sanctuary, pure and holy, tried and true." Oh, it's true. I've heard so many people tell me they don't know how I'm still standing. But I know how I made it. Why I am still standing and I did not give up and I did not allow the fiery darts to penetrate my heart or the adversary's attack cause me to lose my mind. God kept me and I did not let go.

Sometimes, my emotions gets the best of me, and I cry and praise, shout and yell out Thank You Lord for unexpected blessings, unmerited favors, promised provisions, and miraculous miracles. I am a living testimony: protected from rape, delivered from alcohol, saved through a heart operation, forgiven for selfish decisions, guided to the foot of the cross. He has diminished things and people out of my life, just to replenish them with your God' will. God guided the surgeon's hands through brain surgery on my husband, saved our son from a lifetime in prison, blessed our daughter with a gift of a daughter. A position to help people and the gift of being love and to give love. You have blessed us with beautiful grandchildren.

But God, is doing new things in my life. You are giving me confidence, boldness, meekness, hope and new-found faith. Yes, in this preparation you are allowing me to touch lives by letting them know that they might be impacted but not imprisoned. We are losing too many battles because we become offended, unfocused, discouraged, disappointed and loose our determination. Your word clearly tells us in Matthew 6:33 to seek ye first the Kingdom of God and all else will be added. Psalm 23, says, "The Lord is my shepherd I shall no want." Psalm 121 is awesome. It encourages us to lift our eyes unto the Hills from whence cometh our help. Who's that help? Jesus! Beloved, let your hope your peace, joy, love, rest on the solid rock. The rock that will never give away. Trust in the Lord with all thine heart and lean not to your own understanding, but in all thine ways acknowledge him and he shall direct your path. (Proverbs 3:5-6). I cannot begin to tell you how your preparation process is going to be, but one thing I do know is if you don't have a teachable spirit and humble heart, you won't receive the full reward of the preparation process.

During the process, you will have like my grandmother would say "drink tears for water." You will be talked about but still called to show genuine love. You'll at times give up your right for wrong. Now this is a hard one because here you will have to know what the word of God requires of you. Bless those that despitefully misuse you and persecute you. Lord help me, help me. But once you begin to pray about it, practice it, it will become double. I know it is because I've done it time and time again.

Just keep reminding yourself that the Lord is preparing me. I look back over my life and I'm amazed at the blessings the Lord has placed over my life. The biggest preparation is the one of peace. I could remember being this frantic person, every little thing just caused me to be anxious and full of anxiety. If I couldn't find the keys, I got hysterical. If I found the ice tray empty, I would blow up. Not done on my time, I yelled. I'm still working on trying to do it all myself. But the Lord is preparing me. I praise God how He will give me a poem, or I'll be caught by nature. Something he uses to get my attention to analyze what I'm going through at the moment.

AT THE FOOT OF THE CROSS

Notes

CAROLYN BLAKE

Notes

Chapter 6:
The Care Taker

CAROLYN BLAKE

My whole life I have been a caretaker and a nurturer. At twelve years old, I became a financial adviser. When my grandparents' check came, I helped manage the grocery bill, dedicated what was paid to Mr. Jim for carrying us to the grocery store, took out the money for the things that was credited from Parker's grocery. The light bill, Lyner's Cleaners that came to the house for clothes that needed to be dry cleaned. The life of Georgia Insurance, the 97 year-old man that came house to house selling items from the back of his station wagon. Back then, you had home delivery service at budgeted prices and it met their needs and provided much needed services for others in need. Today much of any or everything is for self-gain. Notice I said, "much" not all or everyone. I was the electrician if an extension cord got broken, or the radio or clock did not work right. I even worked on that old Zenith television we had. I even nurtured the appliances.

I was never ever afraid of work. I pumped water, cut wood, washed clothes in a tub or a washboard. We had this washing machine that wrung the clothes between the two rollers. I had a lesson in patience because if you did not put the clothes in right, it would roll itself round and round the roller and then the roller would either get entangled or tear your clothes, or it popped up and at this point you had to pull the clothes off the roller piece by piece. This took patience. The worst part was hanging the clothes on the line. In the summer, gnats and mosquitos tore your arms, neck and legs up. In the winter, your fingers got so cold you could hardly open the pin to hang the clothes on the line. I grumbled like any child would do, but back then, you'd better keep it under your breath or in your mind and with a straight face. In other words, you better not be heard or look like you did not like what you were doing.

Next, I had to make it to my step dad and mom's house on Fridays to make sure I got the money before it was gone. They had an addiction to alcohol, and couldn't manage the money. But, I loved them and they loved us. That is, my two brothers and I did. When my stepdad got paid, he'd always take care of his credit with Mr. Parker who was his brother, then he'll bring some money to momma, a few packages and their little boy.

That's what they called their bottle of Gin. I would get the money for their rent and the light and the life insurance. So actually, in all reality, they did well as long as I got there before it was either lost or taken or given away. I nurtured my brothers, my older brother babysat for the neighbors next door and worked after school and on weekends at Mr. Parker's store. I still laugh when I think about that bicycle with the big basket that he rode from house to house to deliver peoples items they purchased from Mr. Parker's store. My older brother was then a worker and a scholar. First to go to college in the family.

My younger brother was spoiled and I helped him to be that way. He liked animals, especially horses. He also liked to play a lot, but was a good child. He did a lot of sneaky things though and I'd take the blame. Like sneaking sugar and bread and got caught with the sugar on his mouth and said I did not take any. We would go down to Bulowe and pick blackberries and came back and take a cinder block, put broken up tree limbs in each side, sneak the matches, sugar, bread and cream and put the ingredients in the can and on the brick and make blackberry dumpling. See how uncomplicated childhood was? We did not have to go out looking for friends, we were each other's friends. Back then, we created so many imaginary games that we did not have time to think about anything that would bring some one down.

Today, I don't think many children play hopscotch, dodge ball, jump rope, red light green light, marbles, and jack stones. I can remember my cousin and I making our dolls out of a soda bottle and the moss was the hair. These were nurturing times. Even when friends and I had fights, we nurtured our friendship, so much that we fought one minute, and played the next. If they were grudges or hard feelings, you couldn't tell. The community elders were not afraid to tell us right from wrong.

I don't want to make it seem like it was all good, because we had bad days too, but everyone likes to say "I remember when." And even with the bad we should all remember that God is the God of "RE". He restores, renew, revives, replaces, reinstall, and reinstates what a mighty God we serve.

AT THE FOOT OF THE CROSS

Notes

CAROLYN BLAKE

Notes

Chapter 7:
This is my Story

CAROLYN BLAKE

So many times in my life's story, I did not see the hands of God in my situations. The human side of me was in control. Have you had one thing after the other happen in your life? Things that you made an ungodly decision about, but later found out that God had a plan but you gave Him a helping hand. So it didn't work out for your good. Oh, and what about becoming a mother all over again? A cycle that was repetitive, but one you never regret doing because God did it for you. And it was a task, but by His grace He provided for your care and you to care for someone, too.

What about growing up always wondering why alcohol was a part of your family? Drug addiction? Fathers or mothers leaving their children for their own selfish desires? Were you almost or were you molested by a stranger or a family member? Did your family have secrets, known secrets that would have helped if they were exposed? Think back, or not if it affected you in some way along your journey.

The question is, is it still affecting you so much that you are taking it out on yourself or someone else around you? Do you have a spirit of un-forgiveness, a bitterness, hindrance, or low self-esteem? Have you allowed yourself to forgive you or anyone else? It will free you and allow you to dwell in the secret place of the most high where there is healing and peace! I pray that after you've read my experience "At the Foot of the Cross that you will be left feeling that there is hope in life's uncertain circumstances. That God is faithful and He promise never to leave or forsake us.

Life has its ups and downs and we find this out in the book of James. It says, when trouble comes your way count it all joy. But, the sweet thing about it is the verse following it, when your faith is tested and after you endure and go through, your faith will have grown and you will become complete. My story is that I've been tempted, enticed, tried, broken, sick, left to feel lonely, defeated, but if it had not been for God's grace and mercy and me allowing Him to process me, I would not have been able to write this book to encourage my friends, family and others, that God will make a way of escape.

You have to be available to be used by the direction of the Holy Spirit. To have a spirit of wisdom and discernment. To accept the conviction, detection, direction and instruction that God the Revelator will administer to you by being obedient. I can only tell you about my Journey, but a big part of it was my upbringing to know that we are nothing of our own. It is God who works things for our good. (Romans 8:28). He uses us for His good pleasure. In Hebrews 13:8 He's the same today, yesterday and forever more.

You can only find your place in God and allow Him to use you for His Glory. Always have a thankful heart and a humbled spirit. Remain in love with one another, seek peace with each other. I could not end this book without thanking my spiritual mom Mrs. Middleton, for speaking into my life, giving me the two scriptures Psalm 27 and Isaiah 43 and reminding me God will lead me guide me along the way, Lord if you lead me I cannot stray, Lord let me walk, each day with Thee, lead me oh Lord Lead me. My Aunt Rosalie that has been our rock since she said "I Do" to my uncle Daniel Simmons, Sr. who left a legacy behind for us to live by. I thank her for stepping up to the plate to be mom, grandmamma, aunt and so much more to my family and I. Her home is an open home to all she knows. She always used to say, "It's only a house, Heaven belongs to me." God has assigned me another book after this and there's more for you on this life called a journey story. But never forget to cast your cares on God and lay every weight that so easily beset you at the foot of the cross.

CAROLYN BLAKE

Notes

Conclusion

We may have been hurt and thought all was lost, But, I'd like to introduce you to the Cross.

It's at the cross where pain was nailed when you thought that you had failed.

It was at the cross where God took our sins; he bore it all that we may win.

It was on the cross where he hung and bled, so our souls may be saved.

At the foot of the cross we'll find hope and love, joy, and peace.

Grace and mercy but most of all we'll meet the man who set us free, died on the cross for you and for me.

No, we are not lost at the foot of the Cross; there we'll find our burden bearer heavy load lifter, mind regulator.

The one who died on the cross that none may be lost.

Carolyn Blake

CAROLYN BLAKE

Notes

AT THE FOOT OF THE CROSS

Notes

CAROLYN BLAKE

Notes

AT THE FOOT OF THE CROSS

Notes

CAROLYN BLAKE

Notes

AT THE FOOT OF THE CROSS

Notes

CAROLYN BLAKE

Notes

AT THE FOOT OF THE CROSS

Notes

CAROLYN BLAKE

Notes

AT THE FOOT OF THE CROSS

Notes

CAROLYN BLAKE

Notes

Contact Info

Carolynblake698@yahoo.com

Facebook/CarolynEBlake

Order online at amazon.com and all other online distributors

Interested in Writing and or Publishing a BOOK???

Visit:

www.A2ZBooksPublishing.com

www.ingramcontent.com/pod-product-compliance
Lightning Source LLC
Chambersburg PA
CBHW071543080526
44588CB00011B/1776